8/90

FOREWORD

"Frontiers of America" dramatizes some of the explorations and discoveries of real pioneers in simple, uncluttered text. America's spirit of adventure is seen in these early people who faced dangers and hardship blazing trails, pioneering new water routes, becoming Western heroes as well as legends, and building log forts and houses as they settled in the wilderness.

Although today's explorers and adventurers face different frontiers, the drive and spirit of these early pioneers in America's past still serve as an inspiration.

ABOUT THE AUTHOR

During her years as a teacher and reading consultant in elementary schools, Mrs. McCall developed a strong interest in the people whose pioneering spirit built our nation. When she turned to writing as a full-time occupation, this interest was the basis for much of her work. She is the author of many books and articles for children and adults, and co-author of elementary school social studies textbooks.

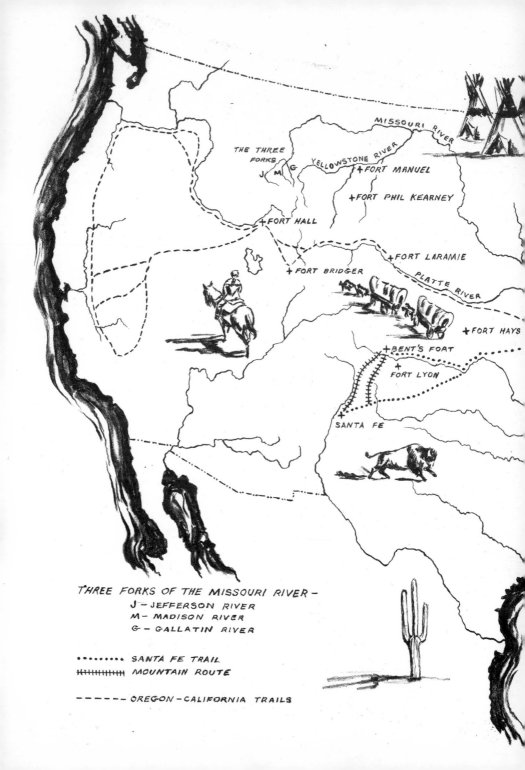

MISSOURI RIVER

THE THREE
FORKS

YELLOWSTONE RIVER

J M G

+ FORT MANUEL

+ FORT PHIL KEARNEY

+ FORT HALL

+ FORT LARAMIE

+ FORT BRIDGER

PLATTE RIVER

+ FORT HAYS

+ BENT'S FOAT
+
FORT LYON

SANTA FE

THREE FORKS OF THE MISSOURI RIVER —
J — JEFFERSON RIVER
M — MADISON RIVER
G — GALLATIN RIVER

•••••••••• SANTA FE TRAIL
⊬⊬⊬⊬⊬⊬⊬ MOUNTAIN ROUTE

— — — — — OREGON-CALIFORNIA TRAILS

INDEPENDENCE

ARKANSAS RIVER

MISSISSIPPI RIVER

Frontiers of America

HEROES of the
WESTERN OUTPOSTS

By Edith McCall

*Illustrations
By William Tanis*

℗ CHILDRENS PRESS ™

CHICAGO

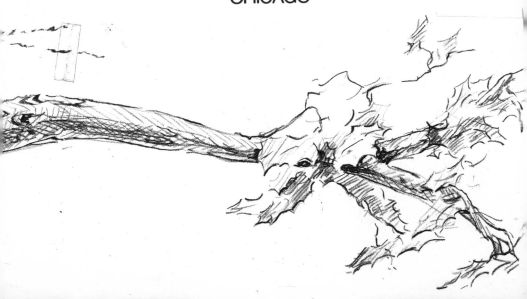

A buffalo-hide shield, Blackfoot

Library of Congress Cataloging in
Publication Data
McCall, Edith S
   Heroes of the western outposts.
   1.   The West—Hist. Juvenile fiction.
a.   Frontier and pioneer life—The West—
Juvenile literature.   I.   Title.
PZ7.Mi229.He   60-11155
ISBN 0-516-03331-X

Cover photograph courtesy
of the National Archives

New 1980 Edition
Copyright© 1960 by Regensteiner
Publishing Enterprises, Inc.
Printed in the United States of America.
   3 4 5 6 7 8 9 10 11 12 R 87

TRUE STORIES IN THIS BOOK

THE FIRST FORT IN THE WEST

Twelve men bent to the work of pulling the big keelboat up the Missouri River. The long rope from the boat passed over each man's shoulder, and was held in the grip of his leathery hands. In turn, the boatmen picked their way over rocks and through overhanging bushes as they moved slowly up the riverbank. The path they followed had been traveled only once before, by the men who went up the long, long river with Lewis and Clark in 1804.

There came a call from the boat.

"Hold fast!" Each man stopped. The current would soon try to move the boat back down the river, and the men braced themselves to hold it steady.

On the deck, a short, dark-haired man looked up the river, turning his spyglass on a small shape which grew larger as he watched it. The man was Manuel Lisa, fur-trader and owner of the keelboat. He was heading up the Missouri River in that year of 1807 to build a fort away up where the river began, where no white man had ever tried to live. In fact, the farthest west settlement in all the land that belonged to the United States was just a few miles west of St. Louis, far down the river from where the keelboat had stopped.

As a man in buckskin leggings and hunting shirt came to his side, Manuel Lisa pointed to the shape on the river. It was plain to see now, even without the glass, that it was a dugout canoe with a lone man in it.

"Look in this glass, George, and see if that is not a white man in that canoe," Manuel Lisa said. He handed his long spyglass to George Drouillard, his guide. George had made this trip up the Missouri with Lewis and Clark three years ago.

George looked through the glass. "It certainly looks like a white man. Mr. Manuel, I believe that is John Colter, the one man we'd like most to see!"

Mr. Manuel, as the men called him, knew that John Colter was the one man who had stayed up the river instead of coming all the way back with Lewis and Clark. He had been alone in the wilderness for more than a year.

"I never thought he'd live through it," said George.

By this time, the man in the canoe was near

enough to call to the men on the keelboat.

"Halloo-oo!"

A moment later, Colter's canoe was alongside the boat. Mr. Manuel and George reached down to shake his hand. John was grinning widely at the sight of his old friend.

Mr. Manuel ordered the keelboat pulled ashore. He had an idea. He talked excitedly to Colter, and when the keelboat moved upriver again, the young adventurer was on board. He was heading back to the wilderness once more.

The keelboat moved on, with the land of the Sioux Indians on either shore. The Indians often came close to the boat in their canoes, but they made no unfriendly moves. Mr. Manuel walked a great part of the journey through the Sioux country. He knew how to keep peace with the chiefs—by going to their lodges with gifts and telling them the reason for the big keelboat's journey through their land.

Beyond Sioux country lay the land of the Aricaras. For a day or two, all was quiet. Very few warriors were seen.

"Too quiet," thought Mr. Manuel. "There should be many Indians in sight."

He soon learned the reason. The boatmen were all on board the keelboat, rowing and poling the boat through water which was not very deep. As the boat rounded a bend, Mr. Manuel saw that they would have to pass through a narrow part of the river. On the riverbanks the warriors were gathered, all in war paint.

George Drouillard whistled. "There must be three hundred of them! What do we do now, Mr. Manuel?"

"I'm not sure, but we'll soon find out," said Mr. Manuel.

As it reached the warriors, the keelboat suddenly faced a flying fence of arrows, shot across the river by the Indians on the banks. Mr. Manuel ordered the keelboat stopped and pulled to the bank.

"Stand by the guns. Fire just once when I signal," he said. Then he walked ashore and directly up to the chief.

The two leaders talked in sign language, and the chief seemed to be saying that his people came in friendship. Then, as if to make it seem that they had come to the river to trade, some of the women brought baskets of corn and set them on the ground near Mr. Manuel.

Mr. Manuel was never sure whether or not a signal passed from the chief to his braves as the white leader looked down at the corn. But suddenly a brave rushed forward and slashed at the baskets with his knife. The women ran away, and each brave fitted an arrow to his bow.

"Fire!" called Mr. Manuel. The guns rang out, and a dozen braves fell. As death hung in the air, Mr. Manuel did not move from his place.

The Indian chief spoke sharply, and the arrows were lowered. The chief made some signs of friendship and one of his braves brought a lighted pipe. It was plain that the Indians would come off second best in a battle between guns and arrows. This man who was the leader showed no fear. Mr. Manuel took the pipe that was handed to him and puffed deeply before he gave it back to the chief. He nodded as the chief made signs that meant "bad man" as he pointed to the brave with the slashing knife.

Mr. Manuel called then for gifts to be brought from the boat. The corn was taken on board, and soon the keelboat moved on.

The Mandan Indian country came next.

"When we came with Lewis and Clark, we spent

a winter with the Mandans," George Drouillard and John Colter told Mr. Manuel. "There should be no trouble at the Mandan villages."

But for some unknown reason, the Mandans, too, tried their tricks against the traders. Again Mr. Manuel stepped from the boat as if he knew no fear. Again the warriors held back.

No keelboat had ever gone higher up the Missouri than the Mandan villages, for Lewis and Clark had sent theirs back from that place. But they had written in their reports that the river was deep enough for keelboats to go two thousand miles up the Missouri. Manuel Lisa planned to take his big boat all the way, if he could continue to pass safely through Indian country.

The keelboat had come a long, long way when it reached the place where the Missouri River makes a sharp bend in what is now the state of North Dakota. There they faced the greatest test of all. Ahead, on an open plain along the river, they saw a great camp of Indians, where Lewis and Clark had not reported any Indian villages.

George Drouillard looked through the spyglass. He said as he passed the glass to Mr. Manuel, "There are three thousand Indians there if there is one."

Mr. Manuel studied the camp for a long time. Then he said, "I would say nearer four or five thousand."

John and George decided, from the horns on the braves' headdresses, that these were a part of the Sioux tribes called Assiniboines. They agreed with Mr. Manuel that there was some good reason for the gathering at the river's edge.

"This calls for a real show," said Mr. Manuel. He called all his men together. Some wanted to go back down the river until this big gathering broke up.

"If we do that, we shall always have to turn back here," Mr. Manuel said. "If there are any of you who want to leave the boat now, do so. But the boat goes on."

No one left. Quietly, Mr. Manuel gave his orders and the keelboat moved ahead. The boatmen did not use the tow rope but worked the boat ahead with the oars and poles and the big square sail. As they drew near the great camp, they saw the Indians gathering as if for battle.

"We must bluff them, or our lives are lost," said Mr. Manuel. All the men who could be spared from the oars and poles were ordered to line up with guns ready. The cannon at each end of the boat was loaded and manned. Then, at a signal from Mr. Manuel, the steersman swung his big "broadhorn" that served as a rudder for the keelboat, and the boat headed directly toward the Indians.

Just outside the reach of an arrow, Mr. Manuel cried, "Fire!" Every gun blazed, and the noise boomed out like a whole season's thunder in one clap. But no Indian fell, for the guns were all pointed over the warriors' heads.

The big boom was still bouncing back from the hills beyond the plain when every Indian had turned his back to the keelboat and was heading for those hills.

"Set poles!" Mr. Manuel called, and the keelboat moved on.

That was the last attack, for just ahead was the mouth of the Yellowstone River, which emptied into the Missouri from the southwest. Mr. Manuel had planned to go as far up the Missouri as the falls that Lewis and Clark had written about, but John Colter thought it would be better to go up the Yellowstone.

"That is Blackfoot Indian country upriver, and

I heard that they were ready to fight the white man. The Crow Indian country is up the Yellowstone. Their land is fine for beaver trapping, and the Crows treated me well last winter. A fur trading post in their country would bring us many beaver skins."

"We can sell all we get," Mr. Manuel said. "As long as gentlemen all over Europe and the United States want beaver hats, there will be a good market for beaver skins."

As the keelboat moved up the beautiful Yellowstone River, there were only wilderness sights and wilderness sounds. It seemed as though no human had ever set foot there. About two hundred miles to the southwest, they reached the place where the Bighorn River empties into the Yellowstone. The journey ended there.

Soon the men who had worked so hard to pull the boat thousands of miles were working just as hard at cutting down trees. They were going to build the first building in what would someday be the state of Montana. They built log cabins and a log stockade around them on the right bank of the Yellowstone, just below the Bighorn's mouth.

They named it Fort Manuel, for the man whose

bravery before the Indians had made it possible for them to reach there safely. It was far, far from any white man's settlement—a lonely outpost in the wilderness.

JOHN COLTER'S RACE FOR LIFE

It took a hero to stay alive in the wilderness around lonely outposts such as Fort Manuel. Sometimes even the heroes took chances that were too big and fell. But John Colter was one of the lucky ones who took big chances and lived to tell his story.

He helped with the building of Fort Manuel. When fall came, it was almost ready as a place to keep men safe and as a center where the Indians would bring furs to trade for the goods Mr. Manuel had brought from St. Louis. But someone had to spread the word that the trading post was there. John was chosen to be the messenger to go to the Indian tribes.

"You know your way in these mountains better than any other man," Mr. Manuel told him. "Carry the word to the Blackfoot Indians as well as the Crows. Tell them we will pay well for all furs they bring to Fort Manuel."

With a pack on his back, his gun and ammunition hung over his shoulder, and his tomahawk and knife in his belt, John set out alone to walk five hundred miles.

At night he cut evergreen boughs to make himself a shelter from the cold winds that swept through the mountain passes. All day he walked through the flame colored woods of the valleys. He saw many wild animals and shot what he needed for food, but no human being moved through the wilderness with him.

The wind was sweeping the tree limbs bare when he found the first tribes of Crow Indians in the upper valley of the Wind River. The Crows were gathering to meet their enemies, the Blackfeet, in war.

John had no choice. He had to fight with the Crows, when the Blackfeet came, or be killed. Before the battle was over, he had an arrow wound in his leg. But worse than that, the Blackfeet Indians had seen him and marked him as an enemy.

John talked with the Crows about bringing their furs to Fort Manuel. Then he headed northeast toward the fort. He had given up further traveling until spring because of his wounded leg and because he knew the Blackfeet would try to kill him.

He walked through deep pine forests. One day he came out of the woods and found himself on the shore of a beautiful mountain lake. Nearby he saw strange boiling springs with clouds of steam rising, not far from the coldest of mountain streams. He watched a great spurt of water rise high into the air. He had happened upon the wonders of what was to become Yellowstone National Park in Wyoming.

When he reached Fort Manuel, winter had set in. He told Mr. Manuel of all he had seen and of the battle between the Crows and the Blackfeet.

"I don't think the Blackfeet will do business with us," he said, rubbing his leg which still pained him.

But some of the men had met a few Blackfeet not far from the fort. "They seemed friendly enough, and interested in trading," Mr. Manuel told John. "In the spring, I would like you to try again, John. Go up to the three forks, where the Missouri River begins, to the heart of the Blackfoot country."

When John set out again in the early spring, two hunters went with him. The three men planned to trap beavers as they went up to the Blackfoot country. John led the way to the country just north and west of Yellowstone Park. They came one day to a fast running river.

"This is the first of the three rivers which meet to

form the Missouri River," John told the other men. "Captain Lewis and Captain Clark named the three rivers after important men in our government. This first fork is the Gallatin. The middle river is the Madison, and the one farthest west is the Jefferson."

"Good beaver sign here," said one of the men, whose name was Potts. "We can trap our way to the headwaters of the Missouri."

The third man, Dixon, decided to trap this stream. Potts and Colter went on to the Jefferson. There they took time to cut down a tree from which to burn and chop out a small canoe. With it, they could paddle up the side streams to set traps.

John's leg was still bothering him. As he rubbed it one night he said, "Potts, every time this leg hurts, I remember the painted faces of those Blackfeet. I don't trust them at all, and I think we'd better be very careful from now on."

One morning, the two men were checking their traps in a small stream which ran into the Jefferson about six miles away. They were in the canoe, moving on to another trap when a sound from the bluffs alongside the stream made them look up.

"Blackfeet!" John said. "Let's get going!"

Potts had the paddle. At the sound of a horrible yell, he pushed for the nearest shore, thinking to run along the valley. But the yelling Indians came sliding down the bank. One of them reached into the canoe and grabbed Potts' rifle.

"Oh, no you don't!" cried John. He leaped ashore and took hold of the rifle at both ends. For a moment, Indian and white man faced each other, testing their strength. Then, with a mighty pull and a grunt, John broke the Indian's grip. He tossed the rifle back to Potts, who was still in the boat.

Potts was too frightened to think. He pushed the canoe out into the stream and began to paddle away. Before he had gone six feet, he screamed and pulled at an arrow in his shoulder.

"Come ashore!" yelled John. "They'd have killed us by now if they wanted to. We'll give ourselves up and see what happens."

But Potts raised his rifle and shot an Indian. As the man fell, a shower of arrows was aimed at Potts. The last John saw of him, he lay in the drifting boat, a dozen arrows in his back.

John turned to his captors. "All right. I'm your prisoner. What are you going to do with me?"

The Blackfeet pulled John to the top of the bluff and ripped off his clothing. From the little he had learned of their tongue, John understood that some of them wanted to set him up as a shooting target. Others seemed to have some other idea.

An older man pushed his way up to John. "The chief," John decided. The braves let go of him as the chief spoke.

Then he turned to John and in sign language asked him, "Can you run fast?"

"What now?" John thought. If he said he could run fast—and he always had been able to outrun every boy and man he raced against—they would expect him to prove it against their best runners. He shook his head and said, "No."

The chief smiled. Then he gave an order to his braves.

"He's going to hold them back and give the poor, slow-running white man a head start," thought John. "So much the better. I'll need every break I can get if I'm to live through this."

The chief took John by the arm and led him about as far away from the waiting braves as one city block would be. All around was the open plain. John was being given the chance to run for his life. Whoever caught him was to have the pleasure of killing him.

"Unh!" said the old chief, and gave John a little shove. John took off at a speed which surprised even himself. Behind him he heard the great war whoop which meant that all the braves who chose to do so were starting after him.

There was no time to pick his way. The open plain was dotted with clumps of a kind of cactus called "prickly pear." John felt the stabbing of its thorns in his bare feet before he had gone one hundred feet. He kept his eyes ahead on his only hope—the dark line, miles away, which marked the grove of cottonwood trees along the bank of the Jefferson River.

Pain was a part of his pounding feet. On and on he ran. He was almost halfway across the six-mile plain before he dared take time to look back over his shoulder. A quick look told him that the main body of Indians was far back, with a scattering of running braves ahead of it. But one Indian, a big fellow carrying a spear, was far ahead of the others. He ran with the stride of a giant, and John felt him gaining on him with each step. He was only about three hundred feet away.

"If I can get to the river—if only I can keep ahead of that one—" John's thoughts brought hope, and his pounding feet somehow went faster. In his chest he felt a pain as if his heart would leap out if it could. Suddenly his nose began to bleed. The warm blood ran down his face and onto his chest. John wasted no motion to try to stop it.

The dark line had grown much clearer, and the fringe of trees began to take form.

"About one more mile," John thought, and took a quick look to see where the big Indian was. What he saw told him that death was on his heels. The man was not more than sixty feet behind him.

A wild idea came into his head. Perhaps he could wrestle the man, and throw him for long enough to kill him with his own spear. All the other Indians seemed to have surrendered their prize to this one man. They were still coming, but more slowly.

His heart told him to keep on running—anything to get away from the man with the spear. His mind told him the spear would bring him down anyway, any second. Courage was all that could save him now.

Suddenly he stopped and wheeled about to face the oncoming Indian. He spread out his arms.

The Indian, only forty feet away, was taken by surprise. John's chest and face were red with blood. At the sight he tried to stop, raising his arm to throw the spear. The suddenness of it all made him trip. He fell, face down. The spear broke as it hit the ground and the Indian's hand held only a broken stick. The spearhead stuck into the ground near by.

John ran for the spearhead and pulled it from the ground. The Indian was trying to get up as John threw himself onto his back. The spearhead cut into the painted skin, and John felt the body grow still.

He felt faint. "I can't—" he thought, but the will to live is strong. In a moment, his tired legs were carrying him toward the river. He knew the other braves had seen what happened and would speed up again.

The cries behind him grew louder as, at last, he reached the cottonwood trees. He plunged on through and into the river.

His heart pounded as he felt the cool water about him. He rested only a moment and then looked for a hiding place.

"I'm in luck," he thought, and began to swim down the river towards an island. At the near end, driftwood had piled up. It floated in the river like an uneven sort of raft.

Drawing on his last bit of strength, John swam to the raft. He ducked under it and swam underwater until he saw a place where his head could be above water between some logs. Over the hole was a covering of smaller branches. He pushed his head and arms into the hole and pulled the small branches around him.

Then, at last, he could rest. His breath came in short, hoarse heaves.

Not three seconds more passed before John heard the first of the Indians rush through the cottonwood trees, screeching and yelling. John could see them searching the bank for signs of him. They followed his tracks to the water's edge. Some swam across and studied the bank on the far side for a long way. Others swam close to him as they headed for the island. Some even stepped onto the raft. John could have touched one with his hand.

"If only they don't set fire to this raft—or pull it apart for firewood," John thought, for he saw that some of the Indians had sat down on the island to rest. What if they should make camp there?

But about sunset all of them returned to the plain. John stayed in his hiding place until darkness had settled. Then, making no more sound than the feeding fish, he swam underwater the length of the island. He waited there a few minutes, listening. Then on he went, still swimming slowly and almost without sound.

When he was well below the island he took less care, but he went a long way down the Jefferson River before he at last climbed ashore. He did not want the Indians to find his tracks in the morning, and chose his spot carefully.

By this time, the chill of the mountain stream had gone through him. The night air was cold, too. Even if he had thought it safe to build a fire, he had nothing with which to do it. Each step on his thorn-ripped, stone-bruised feet was a flash of pain. Half walking, half crawling, he moved slowly in the direction of Fort Manuel.

It was a long, painful journey. John Colter had no clothes, no tools, no weapons, and no food but what his fingers could pull from the earth. The sun of day burned him. The thin, cold mountain air of night was almost more than he could stand. He had to be always on the watch for Indians, grizzly bears or the gray wolf.

After several days, Fort Manuel was before him at last. He stumbled to the gate. The men found him there, more dead than alive.

When he could talk, John told his story. Mr. Manuel listened, able to believe it only because he saw the living man before him.

There was no further thought of going into Blackfoot country. Mr. Manuel headed downriver to take the furs the Crow Indians had brought to the market at St. Louis. John Colter stayed on at the fort, building his strength and trapping in the near-by streams. He did not return to St. Louis until 1810, six years after he had left it to go on the great exploring trip with Lewis and Clark. He went to Captain Clark then, with much to tell him that added to the map of the Louisiana Territory.

Few people believed the story he told. They shook their heads and said, "Man couldn't possibly fight for his life like that!"

But John Colter wasn't an ordinary man. He was a hero.

JOE LA BARGE,
MISSOURI RIVER BOY

After Fort Manuel was built, fur company outposts appeared all along the Missouri River and the rivers which ran into "Old Muddy." The fur business became more important than ever. The posts bought furs from the Indians, and also from the hundreds of white men who went west to become trappers.

St. Louis soon had more fur trading companies. And every boy growing up in the frontier city dreamed of going west to become a fur trapper. One of those boys was Joe La Barge, son of a St. Louis business man. When he was seventeen years old, in 1832, Joe signed up to work for four years for the American Fur Company.

He saw himself heading for the Rocky Mountains with a set of beaver traps and living a life of adventure. But for Joe La Barge, life had other plans.

"You'll be stationed at Cabanne's Post to do whatever work is needed around the post," he was told. He went on board one of the fur company's steamboats and was taken up the Missouri River to a lonely fort on the west bank of the river, about seven miles up-river from where Omaha, Nebraska, is now.

From the start, Joe worked hard to show that he would make a good trapper. His work the first weeks was mostly that of a caretaker and stable boy. Then he was sent to a Pawnee Indian village, about one hundred miles west of the fort, to spend the winter and to buy furs for his company as the Indians brought them in. He handled this work well and was allowed to go down to St. Louis in the summer when the furs were taken to market.

"Now I'll be sent out with a company of trappers," he thought, as he went on board the steamboat to report back to Cabanne's Post.

Joe did not know it, but the Missouri River and the steamboat were to be of greatest importance to him all his life. He was interested enough to learn how the big boat worked as he journeyed up the river. When the crew became ill with a terrible fever and the captain had to go back to St. Louis for more men, Joe was left in charge of the steamboat. He had to pilot it a short distance. But still the life of a trapper was what he looked forward to, and he hopefully returned to Cabanne's as soon as he could.

The trappers were gathering for the fall hunt. Joe listened to their stories of adventure and longed to go with them. But the manager of the post had other plans. He gave Joe important work to do when he could, but he would not let him go with the trappers. He sent him on a journey which he usually trusted only to older men, and praised Joe for work well done, but that was all.

Summer came again, and in the fall Joe was sent to the Pawnee villages on an errand. While he was gone, he had an adventure in which he held off a party of Sioux Indians single-handed.

One of the old-time trappers said to Joe, "You are the kind of young man who would do well in the mountains, Joe. Why don't you join us for the trapping season?"

Joe's eyes brightened. But not for long.

"I need Joe here," the post manager said. "I've got 150 horses here at the post. The company wants them in good shape to go to the mountains in the spring. Joe's job this winter will be to tend those horses."

So the trappers headed for the mountains without Joe. Joe rode herd on the horses as they grazed here and there wherever there was enough grass. When winter came, the manager decided to keep them on the stretch of bottom land across the Missouri River from the post.

Winter's cold winds swept across the river and chilled Joe to the bone. The river began to freeze and Joe could no longer paddle a canoe across each morning and back each night. After an unusually bitter cold night, he found that he could walk across on the ice.

A steamboat had brought a load of feed to the post for the horses but, as winter went on, it was almost gone. No more boats could come upriver until the ice broke in the spring.

"I'll have to cut cottonwood bark," Joe told the post manager one day. Horses could live on cottonwood bark for a short time. He took an ax and a saw with him as he went across the ice that day. He set to work cutting down a cottonwood tree from those that grew close to the river. After the tree was down he cut it into logs from three to four feet long. This was the length the steamboat captains wanted. All Joe needed for the horses was the bark. He stacked the logs near the river's edge for the company's steamboats to pick up in the spring. "Horsewood," the boatmen called it.

One night the men at the post could not keep

warm. They huddled around the fires and talked of adventures they had had in cold weather such as this. The wind whistled through the cracks between the logs all night long, and when morning came the thermometer outside the lodge door read twenty degrees below zero.

"Looks like blizzard weather, too," said the man who had gone out to read the thermometer. "Joe, let those horses take care of themselves today. It's cold enough to freeze your ears off."

Joe had just finished breakfast. "I'd sure like to stay in by the fire today," he said, "but those horses would get too hungry. I'll have to go over there long enough to feed them anyway."

He put on his blanket coat and pulled his leather belt tight around it. He had a fur cap which came down over his ears, and buffalo boots to keep his feet warm, at least for a while. As he tucked his knife and tomahawk into his belt and picked up his rifle, the men by the fire watched him.

"I'd rather fight off a pack o' wild Indians than go tend those horses today," said one.

Joe smiled and waved a mittened hand. "So would I," he thought, "but a job's a job in bad weather as well as good." He pulled the door closed behind him. Soon he was out the stockade gate and heading down the long slope to the river. The first flakes of dry snow were in the air, but with the wind at his back and his collar turned up, the going was easy.

The wind drove him across the ice. He had a regular path he followed. It went between two holes in the ice—"airholes," the men called them. They were about three hundred feet apart.

As he stepped onto the frozen stretch of bottom land, Joe saw that the horses were all huddled together, trying to keep warm. He would feed them and hurry back to the post before the blizzard set in.

"A fire, first," he said aloud. He had a flint box in his pocket. He gathered some rotten wood bits from inside an old stump, and took some chips from where he had been chopping wood. Even against the riverbank, it was hard to build a fire in the strong wind. But at last he had it burning well.

He could turn his back to the wind as he chopped down a tree. That helped a little, but even with the exercise he felt his body growing colder. The clothes which seemed so warm on ordinary winter days couldn't stop the wind. He tried to whistle, but his lips were stiff.

As he quartered the log and started to carry the chunks to his fire, the blizzard set in.

It was hard to see where he was going, but he made the trips to the fire and back as fast as he could. He stood the chunks of wood so that one end leaned against the bank and the fire's heat could reach the bark without scorching it. He had to thaw the bark completely. He went back again and again for more log chunks.

When the first logs had their bark well thawed, Joe took his knife and began the work of stripping the bark from the logs. If any ice were left in the bark, the sharp bits could cut the throat or the stomach of a horse, he had been told. Since he didn't want that to happen, Joe took extra care to pile the bark near enough the fire to keep it from re-freezing. When he had too much to keep near the fire without burning it, he began taking loads up to the horses.

More than once, as the hours went by, Joe thought how much easier it would be to let the horses eat the frozen bark than to fuss with it to keep it free of ice splinters. With one hundred fifty horses to feed, it took a long, long time to do the work. If one died, he could

blame the cold weather. But there was something in Joe's nature that made him do the work as he knew it should be done.

When at last he was through, Joe left the "horse-wood" to stack on a better day and turned toward the river. The full force of the blizzard and the bite of the cold wind hit him. Driving bits of snow blinded him.

"Here goes," he thought, and began to half run across the ice, head down, moving blindly toward the western bank.

Suddenly, Joe felt his foot touch water instead of ice. There was no time to pull back and he plunged into the river. He had run into one of the two airholes.

Even as he was sinking, Joe wondered, "Which one?" If he had fallen into the lower air hole he was lost, for immediately he felt the current pull him down-river. Over his head was a thick layer of ice. If he had fallen into the upper airhole, his only hope was to bump his head along the ice in the hope of finding the lower airhole.

The water closing over him did not bother Joe much. It felt warm after the cold of the air, and he had been swimming underwater for years. Back in the mill pond at St. Louis, he used to swim underwater and grab the legs of a deer as it crossed the pond. He often had killed a deer caught that way and taken the meat and skin home to his family.

Time after time he pushed his head up. Again and again it struck the ice. Then, just as Joe La Barge, best swimmer of old St. Louis, was about to drown for lack of air, his head rose above water. Quickly he reached out with his rifle, which he still held in his right hand, to keep himself from being carried under again and hopelessly down the river.

With his left hand, he reached to his belt and pulled out his knife. A good hard thrust and it was firmly in the ice—a handhold to help him pull his heavy, wet body from the water.

At last he was out and crawling away from the dangerous hole. But as he rose to his feet, he felt the grip of the frigid air. He would soon be an ice figure. He must keep moving, moving . . .

A startled man opened the stockade gate some time later and found the frozen shape of Joe LaBarge fumbling with the latchrope he'd left hanging out. The man half carried, half led the boy to the lodge. Helping hands worked to pull the frozen clothes from an almost unconscious Joe, and to rub some warmth into

him. Later, even when he was wrapped in buffalo robes, Joe's body shook so that the men wondered if he would ever be the same again.

When, at last, he could tell his story, one of the men said, "Your time hasn't come, Joe. Your work remains to be done."

"My work as a trapper," Joe thought.

But Joe never became a trapper. By the time his term with the fur company had finished, the Missouri River, which tried to take his life, called him back. He went to work on one of the steamboats which the fur company owned, and when his time on the boat was up, he had made up his mind. Steamboating was to be his work.

Joe La Barge became one of the best steamboatmen on the Missouri River. He lived through much danger and did many brave things. But he never had a harder day than that wintry one at Cabanne's Post.

THE HERO OF BENT'S FORT

For many years, almost everyone who went west went by way of the Missouri River. But after 1820, a new route began to open. This was a land route and went southwest instead of northwest. It was the Santa Fe Trail.

A few years before the opening of the Santa Fe Trail, a small boy named Kit Carson passed through St. Louis on his way to a Missouri frontier home. Kit's life and the trail would someday become important to each other.

Kit's father, Lindsay Carson, put his family and the few things they had brought west from Kentucky onto the flat, wooden ferryboat that crossed the Missouri River at St. Charles. From St. Charles they headed west along the trail which Daniel Boone's sons had just marked out. It led from St. Charles to the salt springs about one hundred twenty miles to the west. It was called Boone's Lick Road, and most of the American pioneers looking for frontier lands were using it. The Boone's Lick country was as far west as any settlers could go safely. There were forts there, where the settlers could go when Indians attacked.

By the time Kit was fifteen years old, a busy little town had grown up on the Missouri River near his home. Kit's father had died, and his mother decided that Kit should go to that town, called Franklin, to learn a trade.

"Dave Workman wants a boy to help him in his saddle-making shop," she told Kit. It was arranged for Kit to stay with Mr. Workman. Mrs. Carson watched her boy head for town. He didn't look old enough to leave home, even though he was fifteen. He had always been small.

"But he'll get along," she decided, for she remembered the spunk Kit had always shown, and his willingness to try something new.

A year later, Dave Workman had learned to know the boy quite well. He knew that this lad would not long be satisfied with the work of a saddler. Every time a pack train or a wagon train headed west over the Santa Fe Trail, which began in Franklin where Boone's Lick Road ended, Dave saw that dream of going west in Kit's eyes.

He looked over to the bench where the boy was

working. Dave saw the almost fierce way in which Kit brought the sharp-pointed awl down into the piece of leather on which the boy worked. So hard did Kit jab that his long yellow hair fell before his eyes. He dropped the awl impatiently and pushed back his hair.

Just then, sounds of yells and the pounding of hoofs came in through the open door.

"Come on, boy!" Mr. Workman called. "A train's in from Santa Fe!" Man and boy ran out the door, saddle-making forgotten.

Kit and Mr. Workman watched on that April morning in 1826 as the first riders reached town ahead of the train. The men always "lived it up" when they reached Franklin. There was no town in the thousand miles between Santa Fe, New Mexico and Franklin, Missouri. There had been several trading caravans each year since 1821 when Mexico had won its freedom from Spain. In those days, the country that is now the states of Texas, New Mexico, Arizona, Nevada, California, Utah and part of Colorado, with small bits of other western states, all belonged to Mexico.

Several times that summer of 1826, Kit and Mr. Workman, with just about all the other people of Franklin, went out to watch caravans come in or leave.

There were usually a number of wagons, a string of pack mules, and a few horses. When a caravan was heading west, they saw mule teams being hitched to the big wagons, loaded with all sorts of things.

Knives, cloth, pots and pans, needles and pins—the Mexican people wanted almost anything the traders chose to take. They brought back gold, silver, furs and the mules for which Missouri became famous.

Kit was lost in dreams of adventure in the West as he bent over his work in the saddle-making shop. He saw the first steamboats head up the Missouri River, but most of all he was interested in the caravan that followed the Santa Fe Trail. Mr. Workman was not surprised one September day to learn that his young helper had disappeared on the same day that a wagon train had set out for Santa Fe. Some folks said that Mr. Workman helped young Kit get a job helping with the wagons.

Kit's heart was pounding as he mounted the mule he was to ride. Then came the moment when the teamsters snapped their long whips out over the mules' backs, and the trip west began. Mr. Charles Bent, owner of the eighteen wagons, had Kit ride near him

to carry messages to the teamsters from time to time and do odd jobs.

Each night, when the caravan camped, Kit sat near the fur trappers who were traveling with the train. He heard the stories the men told of their adventures in the Rocky Mountains. That was the life for him! Kit would become a trapper as soon as he reached the Great West.

One bright November morning, Kit saw the white adobe buildings of Santa Fe. The sunshine on the walls almost blinded him. As the caravan entered the old, old city, dark-haired, brown-skinned children ran alongside, crying out in excitement.

His work finished, Kit set out to prove that, small as he was, he could be a mountain man. He got work cooking for a band of trappers. It was months before he had a chance to prove that he could set traps and be a real trapper. The other trappers thought he was too small to open the jaws of the heavy traps, and Kit had to show them that he was tough, even though he was small.

Five years later, he had proved it well. He was becoming known as one of the best of the trappers. He could live for months at a time with no roof over his head, eating what he could find or kill for himself. The bundle of beaver furs he brought in was as large as anyone's, and larger than most.

He always made his way back to the country just north of Santa Fe, and often brought his furs to his old friend, Trader Charles Bent or Charles' brothers. The Bent brothers had chosen a place on the mountain route of the Santa Fe Trail to build a trading post right after Kit had come west with Charles.

When Kit went south from the Big Horn River country in 1829, he found the Bent brothers building a fine, new trading post on the Arkansas River. Their earlier outposts had log walls, but this one was to be different.

"I want a fort which can't be burned down," Charles Bent told Kit. Kit went down to Taos with Charles and saw the Mexicans at work making "adobe" —large clay building blocks, sun-baked to the hardness of stone. Some of the workers were mixing sheep's wool in the muddy clay with their feet.

"What is that for?" Kit asked.

"They usually put straw in the clay, as it helps to hold the clay together," Charles told him. "But wool makes even stronger adobes."

Kit spent a great deal of time around the new trading post as it was being built. He became a good friend to William Bent, who was in charge of the post. Charles was gone on trading trips most of the time.

In 1832, Kit found that Bent's Fort was finished at last. He rode in from a season's trapping and was surprised to see how big the place was. William Bent was proud to show him around.

"Those outside walls must be six feet thick at the base," Kit exclaimed. "How high are they? And how long is that side wall?"

Colonel Bent told him, "It took a lot of adobe to build those walls. They're fifteen feet high, six feet thick at the base and two feet at the top. This east wall, with the main gate, is one hundred thirty feet long. The front part is square, but the side walls reach back to the west an extra fifty feet for the corral on the back."

The corral walls were lower, but their tops had big, prickly cactus growing in them. Kit was sure no one would try to climb over them. He was especially interested in the two thirty-foot high round towers at the southeast and northwest corners of the main part of the fort.

"There are cannons in the upper room," the colonel told Kit. "We can fire in any direction from them."

They went through the big wooden gates. The whole outside face of the gates was covered with nailheads. The first thing Kit saw in the courtyard was a big cannon facing the gate. This was a real fort, he thought, strong enough to hold off any enemy. Above the big gate was a watchtower.

"Someone is always up there, with a spyglass," Colonel Bent said. "I knew you were coming when you were a long way off. That is how I could come out to meet you."

Later, Kit had a new experience. He sat in the game room, built above the rooms on the west wall of the fort, enjoying a cold drink on a hot summer day. For Bent's Fort even had an ice house, stocked with blocks of ice cut from the Arkansas River on a cold winter day.

"Imagine that!" Kit said. "Not another building for hundreds of miles, and here we are living like the rich fellers back in St. Louis!"

Kit came back to Bent's Fort whenever he could.

The fall of 1832, he was with a company of trappers not far from the big fort. It was about this time that

Kit began to do the bold things for which he became well known.

It was a cold January morning in 1833, and the wind was howling through the valley where Kit and his trapper friends were camping. The men awoke to discover that nine of their horses had been stolen in the night.

Kit studied the tracks left in the snow. "I reckon there were about fifty Indians in the party—likely Crows. Let's get going. Got to get those horses back."

Soon he and eleven other men were on horseback following the snowy trail. By the time darkness came, they had gone about forty miles. Their horses were tired, as the going was hard through deep snow. So many buffalo herds had crossed the trail that it had been easy to make a wrong turn, and much time had been wasted.

"See that grove of trees over there?" Kit asked. He pointed to a dark ridge, two or three miles away. "We'd better make camp there."

The men headed for the grove. They tied their horses to trees well inside the grove.

"Now for some rest," one of them said.

But Kit's eyes had picked up a distant glow, off in

the direction where the great shape of Pike's Peak arose. "No, sir, we'll not rest. There is the Indian camp. Can't be more than three or four miles from here. We'll go and get our horses before we rest."

One of the men started for his horse.

"No," said Kit, "we'll have to walk. They'll see us coming if we ride, and we've got to surprise them. After all, there are about fifty of them and only twelve of us."

The men left their horses in the grove and set out. They circled around to keep in the shadows and to not cross the open fields of snow. When they were still some distance from the camp, they dropped to their knees and crawled the rest of the way. In all, it took them about four hours to reach the Indian camp.

About three hundred feet from the camp, they stopped to make plans. They could see two big camp-fires, with Indians dancing around them, singing as they danced. They had built two protecting circles of brush—"forts," Kit called them.

"They're happy because they think they got away with our horses," Kit whispered. "We'll fix them. Those look like our horses, tied just this side of the first fort."

"How will we get them?" asked one of the trappers.

Kit whispered, "Lie quietly here until they go to sleep. Then, six of us will creep up on them and six wait here." He chose his six men.

The cold of their snowy resting place had gone clear through to the men's bones before the Indian camp was finally quiet. Kit raised his arm as a signal and began to creep toward the captured horses. They were glad of the snow then, for the six men could crawl without making a sound. They stood up only when they were close to the horses. Still without speaking, they cut the ropes and tossed snowballs at their horses to start them moving away from the Indian camp.

"Let's get out of here," one of the men whispered when all twelve men were back together with their horses retaken. He was already climbing onto the back of one of the horses.

"And let those Indians off free when we had to go to all this trouble?" Kit seemed surprised the man would think of leaving so soon.

"We got what we came for. Let's go," said one of the men.

But Kit would not leave. He was going to punish

the Indians. He said, "They'll think we've gone soft. Come on, now. Who's for teaching them they can't steal our horses?"

"I'm with you, Kit," said one. In a few moments, all twelve men had agreed to try to punish the Indians. Three of them took the horses back to the grove where the others were tied. Nine crawled back to the Indians' "fort."

A dog in the Indian camp barked, and in a moment the camp had come to life.

"Get them!" hissed Kit, and his men opened fire. The first Indians fell.

The first glow of morning light was on Pike's Peak by this time. Kit and his men were careful to stay behind trees as they reloaded their guns. The Indians had begun firing, too, and a real battle was on. The Indians stayed inside their brush forts, never dreaming that only nine trappers would have the courage to attack fifty Indians.

The battle was still going strong when full daylight came. The Indians then found out what a small party was firing at them. They charged from their forts, thinking to make quick work of the men behind the trees. A wild yell filled the air.

"Hold your ground, men!" Kit called out, and each trapper brought down one Indian. The other Indians dropped back to their fort again, and there was quiet for a few minutes.

"Let's get out of here, Kit," said a trapper.

But Kit was not ready. "One more charge," he said.

So the nine men waited. But the next time the Indians, too, shot from behind trees. Even Kit saw that the fighting could go on a long time, and it would be wise to begin backing away before their ammunition ran out.

"Move towards camp, but keep on firing," he ordered.

Running from tree to tree, and yelling wildly, the trappers drew the Indians after them. But not one trapper fell. When the trappers were not far from where their horses and the other three men waited, the Indians gave up and dropped back.

"Good enough," said Kit. "That'll teach them not to sneak up on us in the night and take our horses. Let's go!"

Back to their main camp they went, without having had a bit of sleep for almost thirty hours.

At the end of the season's trapping, Kit went back to Bent's Fort. The story of his adventure had gone ahead of him. Kit Carson was becoming known as one of the bravest of mountain men. A few years later, when he became the chief scout and guide for Captain John Fremont's exploring and map-making company, he became known all over the United States. True stories were told about him, and adventure story writers made up many more with Kit Carson as the hero.

For twenty years, Bent's Fort stood on the mountain branch of the Santa Fe Trail. Thousands of travelers, Indians and white men alike, came there to trade or to rest awhile. Many of them met Kit Carson there, and they always remembered the little man with the big share of courage.

LONG JOURNEY TO THE FORT

Charles Bent was bringing another caravan of trading goods to the big fort on the Arkansas River. Almost ten years had passed since the journey on which Kit Carson had come west with him, but Charles thought of that journey often as the caravan moved along. He had another boy with him, much like Kit. This boy, James Hobbs, was heading west for a life of adventure, just as Kit had done in 1826.

Like Kit, James was almost too eager to rush into adventure. On a morning when a few buffalo came near the caravan, James' eagerness got him into trouble. A second boy, John Baptiste, followed wherever James led. So he, too, fell into trouble.

When the buffalo came near, James tried his hand at shooting a few, along with the older men. He was lucky and brought one down. One of the animals became frightened and ran towards the end of the caravan as it moved along on the north bank of the Arkansas River.

"Get her, buffalo boy!" some of the men yelled to James.

James had been reloading his pistol. It was really too small for buffalo hunting, and his shot only wounded the stray buffalo. She charged toward the end of the caravan, cut across the Santa Fe Trail and crossed the Arkansas River. James, with John following him, charged after her.

"Let her go!" Mr. Bent called to James.

But James was sure that one more shot would bring her down. He spurred his mule on and called over his shoulder, "I'll get her and then catch up with the train, Mr. Bent! Come on, John! Help me get her!"

A moment later, the two boys were charging through the river. It was not deep, and their mules were soon on the other side. But the buffalo was well ahead of them. Her wound made her run faster instead of slowing her down. James knew he should turn back, but he hated to face the teasing of the men if he came back without this buffalo's hide.

On and on went the chase until the boys were three miles from the trail. Even then the buffalo put up a fight, and the boys circled around her several times before she fell.

"Got her!" James yelled. He jumped from his mule. "Help me skin her, John, and we'll take the hide and a couple of nice roasts back to the train."

As they worked, John looked at the sky. The sun had disappeared, and darkness was coming fast. "We'd better hurry," he said. "There's no moon tonight, and it will soon be too dark to see where we are going."

"Don't worry," said James. "We'll just head back the way we came. "When we come to the river we'll cross it, and follow along it until we come to the night's camping place."

They skinned the buffalo, taking a long time because it was new work to them. Then they packed some good hump meat into the hide and tied it onto one of the mules.

"I think the sun set over that way," John said then. "That means we should keep that direction at our left to go north to the river."

James was looking about. "I'm not so sure," he said. "That doesn't seem right to me. You turned around so many times since the sun set that I don't see how you can tell where it went down."

James began moving the opposite way from that which John wanted to go. He got down on his knees and carefully felt about in the sandy soil where the mules had walked. "I can tell by the tracks," he said. "We'll go the opposite way from these tracks."

The boys got onto their mules and began to ride. They rode on and on, but they did not come to the river, for James had forgotten how they had circled around the buffalo before bringing her down. Morning's first streak of light was to their left, and they knew they must be far from the Santa Fe Trail.

"May as well cook some of this meat before we head back," James said. The boys got off their mules and unloaded the meat pack. They built a fire near the edge of a ravine, and rested while the meat cooked. It had been a long night.

Both fell asleep. They were awakened by the pounding of hoofs passing them.

"Buffalo!" yelled John. He jumped up and reached for the hide and the rest of the meat to put it onto his mule.

"Never mind the meat, John. Indians are coming!" cried James, and he headed for the ravine.

John turned and saw a band of about fifty Indians riding after the buffalo herd. He, too, dropped down into the ravine.

But they were too late. A moment later, about a dozen Indians were peering down at them from the ravine's edge. They called and motioned to the boys to come up.

"Let's bluff it out, John," whispered James. "We can't escape, so act brave and friendly."

They climbed back up and faced the Indians. To their surprise, the Indians acted quite friendly.

"How d' do?" said one.

James answered, "How d' do."

"Texas?" the Indian asked.

James was glad he had kept his ears open when he was with the trappers and had learned that most Indians hated the Texans.

"No, we're not from Texas," he said. "Friendly."

The Indian who could speak English grunted, "Tobacco?"

James pulled some from his pocket and handed it to the Indian. He guessed these were Comanches, and later learned he was right.

The Indian looked pleased. He motioned to the

boys to get their mules. "Ride with us," he said.

James and John thought it best to do as asked. Soon they were riding towards the larger group of Indians, going farther from the Santa Fe Trail with each step. At the end of the day, they rode into a large camp where about a thousand Indians were gathered. They were shown to a lodge for the night.

About noon the next day, the chief, Old Wolf, was ready to decide what to do with the two boys. The English speaking Indian came for them. As they reached the chief's lodge, he pointed to some dried scalps hanging on a pole.

"Mexicans," he said. "Comanches give them lodging, let them care for ponies. They try to run away."

James and John remembered that short lesson. Old Wolf was willing to let them join in the life of the tribe. When the tribe moved on, James and John went along, planning to wait for their chance to get to Bent's Fort.

Life with the Comanches was an adventure to James. Soon he was riding on the hunt with the Indians.

"You make fine brave," Old Wolf told him. But he had little to say for John, who longed only to finish the journey to Bent's Fort.

A year passed and then another. At the end of the third year, Old Wolf gave his daughter to James to be his wife. James felt himself almost as much Indian as white man when another year had passed. He had almost forgotten about Bent's Fort when he heard an Indian speak of it.

The Comanches and Cheyennes had met at a place called *Big Timbers* for a great feasting. The braves of the two tribes played games and held races, each trying to outdo the other. The Comanches won most of the horse races. Since the prize for winning a race was the pony of the loser, the Comanches ended the feast with many extra ponies.

"Trade them at Bent's Fort," one of the Cheyennes suggested. "Colonel Bent will pay you for horses. We go there each year with deerskins and furs to trade."

Old Wolf thought about this. Then he decided that, since Bent's Fort was not far away, he would go there with the Cheyenne chief.

A new excitement arose in the hearts of James and John. Would their journey to the fort end at last? Looks passed between them, but they said nothing.

Ponies were mounted. The women packed the camping gear onto poles tied to other ponies' sides, and the Indians all set out for the big adobe fort on the Arkansas. They joined the hundreds of other Indians who were camping on the plains around the fort and set up their skin lodges.

Old Wolf had never been inside the fort. He asked his white son-in-law to go with him as the Cheyenne chief led them to the big gates. William Bent, Kit Carson, and a trapper named John Smith met them there.

"You are welcome to my lodge," William Bent told the chiefs. Then he stared at James. Was this painted fellow white or Indian?

James waited for his chance to talk to William Bent alone. "I came west with your brother, Charles," he said. "Perhaps he told you, a long time ago, about the foolish boy who didn't obey when he was told not to chase a buffalo? I'm that foolish boy. My friend, John Baptiste, who went with me, is in the Indian camp outside the fort."

William held out his hand. "I do remember," he

said. "Charles wondered for a long time what had become of you. He was afraid you had been killed."

James knew at the touch of Colonel Bent's hand that he wanted to be with his own people again. He saw other Indian women moving about the fort, and knew that he could bring his Indian wife there to live with him. It was journey's end at last for him and for John.

The next day, Old Wolf was shown all the wonders of the great adobe fort. When a cannon in one of the round towers was fired with a blank charge, he hurried back down. Outside the walls, his people thought he had been killed. When they got over their fright at the roar of the gun, they came to the walls and cried out that they wanted to see their chief.

"Old Wolf is well," James told them. "Soon the trading will begin."

When Old Wolf saw all the fine goods in the storerooms, his eyes opened wide.

William Bent said, "You see, Old Wolf, it is well to be the white man's friend. We have much here that you want, and big guns to keep us safe. Come to us in peace and friendship, and we shall be as brothers. And now, I would like to give you some gifts for bringing my white sons back to me."

Old Wolf looked sadly at James. "You not want to be Comanche brave?" he asked.

James said, "I will always be brother to Comanche, but my people are here."

Old Wolf grunted. He quickly agreed to give up John in exchange for an old mule. But for James he had to have more. Colonel Bent gave him a full pound of tobacco, an ounce of bright-colored beads, and what he wanted most of all—six yards of bright red flannel cloth.

The trading table at the corral gate was set up then, and the goods brought out for trading for the ponies, deerskins, buffalo robes and furs which the Indians had brought. The Indians were ordered to form a line and the trading began. It went on for eight days. The Indians wanted guns, ammunition, knives and tobacco, but they were also pleased to get such things as tin whistles, spoons, mirrors and bright cloth.

When the Comanches and the Cheyennes rode away, James and John watched them go. James' Indian wife stayed on at the fort, too.

Kit Carson became James' hero, and the younger

man asked to go with Kit to learn to trap. Kit liked the boy and let him join him when he and a party of trappers left Bent's Fort that fall.

On that first trip, James saved the life of one of the trappers who was attacked by a grizzly bear. Kit Carson shook the young man's hand.

"You have the makings of a mountain man, James," he said. "I'm mighty glad you finally ended that long journey to Bent's Fort!"

JIM BRIDGER, MOUNTAIN MAN

At the same time that Kit Carson was growing up near Franklin and Joe La Barge was the champion swimmer of St. Louis, young Jim Bridger was living in St. Louis, too. Jim longed to go west, just as the others did.

There was no time for sport in Jim's boyhood days. His family was poor. To feed his children, Jim's father ran a ferryboat across the Mississippi River and worked as a blacksmith on the riverfront between trips. He died when Jim was thirteen years old, and the boy took over the hard work his father had done.

He saw the keelboats being loaded for the trips to the trading posts far up the Missouri River. He heard the stories, told year after year, of those who had gone with Lewis and Clark and of the men who had been at the faraway outposts. His tired arms kept on swinging the blacksmith's hammer and the clang of iron on iron filled the shop with sound. But in Jim's heart he was setting beaver traps and the sound was the laughter of the merry mountain men.

"I'm going," he decided one day when he was eighteen years old. Colonel William Ashley's keelboats were ready to leave for a trip to the forks of the Missouri River. Mike Fink, strongest keelboatman of them all, was in charge of the boat crews. He wore a red feather in his old felt hat as a sign that he could "outrun, outhop, outjump, knock down, drag out, and lick any man in the country."

When Mike bellowed, "Set poles for the mountains!" Jim Bridger was on board one of the boats. He had signed up for three years in the mountains, and he felt as if his life was beginning anew.

Young Jim learned a great deal those first years. And one of the hardest things he had to learn was how to be a hero, to others and to himself.

An accident to one of the keelboats kept Colonel Ashley and his partner, Major Henry, from going all the way up the Missouri River. The men went trapping around the Yellowstone River, instead. They built small forts to which the men went back with their furs after short trapping trips.

Jim Bridger was learning the work of a trapper fast. An old mountain man named Hugh Glass had taken him "under his wing" and shown him many of the things a man had to know in order to catch beaver. On Jim's second year in the West, he and Hugh Glass were both in a party of men under Major Henry. They were on their way back to one of the small forts with their catch when a great grizzly bear attacked old Hugh Glass.

Hugh was ripped and crushed by the bear. He lay near the mountain trail, still alive but very, very weak.

"I don't see how he can possibly live," Major Henry said. "And he is too weak for us to take him with us. Yet we must move on. But Hugh has been a good friend to many of us and we cannot leave him to die alone. Are there two men who will stay with him until he dies and then bury him?"

The men looked from one to another, but no one spoke. The mountain pass was a lonely one, with danger all around. There were more grizzly bears, but even worse, it was believed that an enemy Indian tribe was near by.

"It will only be for a day or so," Major Ashley said.

Young Jim Bridger, in the silence that followed, remembered how good Hugh Glass had been to him. "I'll stay," he said. But not another man spoke up.

"There'll be extra pay for the man who will stay," said Major Henry.

A new man with the company spoke then. "I'll stay." His name was Fitzgerald. If Jim had been choosing his company, he would have left Fitzgerald to the last.

The rest of the men moved on. Jim sat beside Hugh Glass by the hour, doing all he could for the old trapper. Fitzgerald went hunting and brought in food for them. The day passed, and a long night in which the wolves howled. The morning light came, and Hugh Glass was still alive. Slowly that day, too, went by.

"Look, boy," Fitzgerald said that night, "he can't last much longer. As soon as it's light enough, let's me'n'you get going before the Indians find us."

"We said we'd bury Hugh before we left," Jim said. But even he had begun to wonder how much longer the wounded man could hold on.

In the morning, Hugh's heartbeat was very, very weak.

"Come on, kid, let's go," said Fitzgerald. "How we going to catch up with Major Henry?"

"We can find our way to the fort, and he can't hold

out much longer," said Jim. "We must wait until he dies."

Fitzgerald went out hunting again. When he came back he began to pick up his belongings. "We're getting out of here or there'll be three dead men instead of one," he said. "I heard the war cry of an Indian party. I'm not waiting. We'll tell them Hugh died and we buried him. No one will ever know the difference."

He walked over to Hugh and picked up the wounded man's knife, his tomahawk, his rifle and ammunition. "He'll never need these and no use leaving them for the Indians," Fitzgerald said, and began to walk away.

Jim stood a moment. Hugh seemed scarcely to be alive at all. He thought of staying on alone and a wave of sickness went through him. He turned his back on Hugh and ran after Fitzgerald.

"I knew you'd be sensible," the older man said.

For many weeks, Jim dreamed each night, seeing the face of Hugh Glass, torn by the claws of the big grizzly. But Hugh's eyes were always open, and they looked at Jim with a look that made him awaken with cold sweat standing on his brow. He grew thin and the other men asked him if he felt well.

Jim was glad when Fitzgerald left the fort. It helped not to have the man around as a reminder of the secret they shared. Months passed, and Jim began to sleep better and to take more part in the joking among the men.

One day, Jim rode in from a day in the woods near the fort. He put his horse in the corral and turned to follow the stockade wall to the fort gate. Darkness was coming, and he couldn't decide who the man was who was coming toward him. The fellow walked with a limp, and Jim knew no one at the fort who limped.

The man came straight toward Jim. He said not a word but reached for Jim's throat. Jim felt his head banged against the stockade, and he couldn't breathe. He stared at the stranger who was bent on killing him. And then Jim knew. That scarred, ugly, gray-whiskered face was that of a man come back from the dead— Hugh Glass! He tried to cry out.

"You know me, don't you?" Hugh said. "Yes, it's old Hugh, come back to haunt a man who would leave him to the wolves and the Indians!" But as he spoke, he loosened the grip of his fingers, and Jim could breathe again.

Jim knew he should be frightened when Hugh said, "I'm going to squeeze the life out of you, my black-hearted friend!" But the feeling that came to him was joy. Hugh had not died there, alone in the mountain pass!

He said, "Go ahead, Hugh. Kill me. I have it coming, and I've died a hundred times since we left you. But I'm glad you're alive, Hugh Glass!"

Hugh's arms dropped to his side. He stared at Jim for a full minute. Jim did not try to run.

"I do believe you are glad," Hugh said at last. He turned and walked to the gate. Jim followed.

Jim learned later the almost unbelievable tale of how Hugh had grown better instead of worse, how he had crawled to water, and then, when his strength came back a little, had begun a journey on his hands and knees which brought him finally to an outpost on the Missouri River. His razor had been left in his pack, and with it he had got food for himself and somehow kept alive. At the fort, willing hands had cared for him until he had set out to find the men who left him to die alone.

Jim had to prove to the other men and to himself that he would never do again the kind of thing he had done to Hugh Glass. He faced danger time and time again without backing off. He became so good a trapper that Tom Fitzpatrick, one of the owners of the Rocky Mountain Fur Company, made him his "right hand man."

He explored a great deal. Jim was the first to see Great Salt Lake. He and Tom Fitzpatrick found the pass through the mountains which was known as South Pass and was later used by thousands of people traveling in wagon trains to Oregon or California. Jim visited Yellowstone Park, as John Colter had done, and reported the many wonderful things to be seen there.

By 1840 Jim Bridger was known far and wide as one of the best trappers, scouts and guides that ever lived. Indian chiefs knew when they met him that he was fair and brave. But, like Kit Carson, Jim saw that a trapper's life no longer paid. The beavers were almost gone, and, too, beaver hats had gone out of style. He had to find something new to do.

One summer day in 1840, Jim Bridger and Tom Fitzpatrick were sitting in the courtyard at Fort Laramie. Fort Laramie was one of the larger posts the fur company had built on the third trail which opened to the west—the trail which went from Independence, Missouri, westward and a little north, following along the Platte River.

"Another wagon train coming in," said Jim. "More and more folks are heading out for Oregon."

"Five years ago, there weren't more'n fifty Americans out there all told," Fitzpatrick said. "Must be hundreds of them out there now."

They went to the gate. Fort Laramie stood on a rise, on the north bank of the North Fork of the Platte River. They counted sixteen wagons making camp outside the fort walls. As soon as they had their cattle tended to, the people would be coming into the fort. They had come along five hundred miles of trail since the last time they had had a roof over their heads.

"Can't blame them for feeling happy to be here," said Fitzpatrick, "but I don't suppose they have any idea of the rough going that's ahead of them. They have mountains and desert all the rest of the way."

Jim Bridger said, "And this is their last chance to get supplies and a bit of rest—except for Fort Hall, 'way over in the Snake River Valley."

Jim thought more and more about the long distance on the trail without shelter for the people who were traveling to Oregon or California. A couple of days later, he saw these sixteen wagons leave Fort Laramie with Tom Fitzpatrick going along as their guide, and he felt sure they'd get through the mountains. But there wasn't always an old mountain man as good as Fitzpatrick ready to guide them.

"You know, a fellow could make money and help people at the same time if he opened up a post farther on to the west," Jim told a friend. "I'm going out to a spot I know on Black's Fork of the Green River, on the other side of South Pass. I'll build a fort there, and folks will be mighty glad to stop awhile."

When the big wagon trains of 1843 came by, Jim had Fort Bridger finished. The old work he had done as a blacksmith came back to him, and he put new shoes on many a horse and mule that was crossing the mountains. The fort had a carpenter shop where wagons could be fixed, and a store where travelers could buy supplies.

The land around Fort Bridger was good for growing vegetables, and travelers could have their first fresh food in many a week. When a wagon train arrived, there was usually a side of beef or pork ready, as a change from Buffalo meat.

That year of 1843 was the real beginning of the great wagon trains to the west. The outposts were no longer needed for the fur trade, but they became the most important places on the trails to those who were crossing the plains and the mountains.

Jim Bridger sometimes visited with the folks who stopped at his post, but often the travelers did not see the old mountain man. He was too restless to stay at the fort for long. His part in the opening of the west was not yet over.

THE WAGON TRAIN RAID

The trails westward grew hard and wide from the iron-rimmed wheels of hundreds and hundreds of big, white-covered wagons. The more travelers there were, the more supplies were needed at the outposts. Supply wagon trains went back and forth from the Missouri towns to the outposts, adding to the traffic over the trails.

One day in June of 1845, four trappers still trying to make a living from furs, reached a bluff overlooking the Santa Fe Trail. They had been in the mountains for three years, and had at last collected enough beaver, otter, mink and other furs to take them to market. They planned now to follow the old trail to Missouri. They made camp on the grassy plain above the bluff, and cooked their evening meal. Their five pack mules were hobbled and taken to feed near the edge of the plain.

Supper over, the trappers leaned against some large rocks and filled their pipes with tobacco. But the mules began to snort and try to break loose from their hobbles. John Smith, one of the trappers, got up to look around.

"Mules don't act like that unless there's something in the wind," he said. He walked to the edge of the bluff and looked down at the trail below, with the Arkansas River just beyond it. As far as he could see, nothing was in sight.

He went back to the rocks near the campfire where his three friends, Dick, Al and Bill, waited.

"Nothing in sight, but I wouldn't be surprised if something came along the trail soon," he said and settled down again. The men had made camp early, and it was still light.

The sun had dropped halfway out of sight when the mules became too noisy for the men to overlook. All four trappers were going towards the bluff's edge when a shot and the sound of Indian war cries reached their ears.

This time, the trail was not empty. A long line of wagons, heading to the east, was trying to get into circle formation to protect itself. A band of about sixty Pawnee Indians rode around the wagons, shooting arrows into the circle.

"Come on, boys!" yelled John. All four men had

picked up their rifles, just from habit, as they headed for the bluff. They scrambled down the steep slope.

The last of the wagons had dropped behind by almost a quarter of a mile, and now it was hopelessly cut off from the rest. With a great war whoop, several of the Indian riders headed for it. The trappers saw a man, a woman and a small boy jump down from the wagon and begin to run towards the other wagons.

"They need help, boys!" John yelled. He and his friends ran towards the little family. Before they were near enough to fire their rifles at the Indians, they saw the man fall. The woman and the boy were ahead of him, but the Indians did not shoot at them. Instead, two of them rode their ponies toward the racing woman and child.

One of them reached the woman. He reached down and pulled her onto the pony, holding her before him. Then he wheeled about and headed back to the west.

The other Indian was just about to swoop up the boy when Al's rifle rang out. "Bang!" The Indian fell from his pony and the boy ran on toward the trappers.

Dick reached him first. He picked up the child, who was about seven years old, and ran with him

toward the circle of wagons. The other three men fired
at Indians who aimed at Dick as he ran. With their
help, he made it safely inside the circle. John, Al and
Bill fought their way inside, too, and took places
beside the wagon men.

The battle did not last long, for darkness came
and brought it to a stop. The Indians rode off to the
west.

"They may come back to surprise us in the night,"
the trappers told the wagon men. "We'd like to break
camp and head east with you folks, if you don't mind."

John Smith looked for the little boy. He found

him sitting right where Dick had put him. By that time, the trappers had learned that this was a Mexican wagon train taking mostly empty wagons to Missouri to bring back the parts for a sawmill. The boy belonged to an American family which had asked to travel with them. None of the Mexicans so much as knew his name.

"We'll fix you a bed in one of the wagons, lad," John said to the boy. He gathered blankets from all those who could spare them and put them into the wagon which would be in the middle of the train. All had agreed that they should travel on all night to put as much distance as they could between themselves and the Indians.

"You'll be all right now, boy. Uncle John will take care of you," said the trapper. He patted the boy gently and turned to go. The frightened look in the lad's eyes upset him.

Al, Dick and Bill were already up on the plain putting the pack saddles and packs onto the mules. They brought the mules down to the trail and then helped round up the cattle the wagoners were driving to Missouri to sell. It was about ten o'clock when the wagon train rolled forward once more.

All night the drivers kept the tired animals moving on. When daylight came and there was no sign that they were being followed, they found a place where there was good grass for the animals. Then at last they stopped.

John went to the wagon where he had put the boy. The little fellow was still asleep. The trappers built a fire and cooked some breakfast. John went back to the wagon and found the boy just waking up.

"Come on, son. Time to eat," the trapper called. The boy had a wondering look on his face, as if he did not know where he was or how he came to be there.

But he spoke for the first time since his rescue from the Indians.

"Where's my mama?" he asked.

John hardly knew what to say. He did not have much hope that the boy's mother had lived through that night, and less that the boy would ever see her again. But he said, "We'll find her, son. Come now, let's wash your hands over at the river and then get some food into you. Aren't you hungry?"

The boy went with John to the river. As he washed the child's face, John asked, "What's your name, son?"

"Paul," said the boy.

"Paul who? Do you have another name?"

"Paul Dale. What's your name, mister?"

John said, "You can call me Uncle John, Paul."

Paul was hungry and ate a good meal. Afterwards, he came close to "Uncle John."

"Uncle John, where's mama?" he asked again.

John did not know what to say. "She's gone for a while, but we'll find her someday," he told Paul. The boy nodded. Then John saw Al bringing the mules up from the river. "How would you like to ride on a mule, Paul?" he asked.

Paul was pleased. He ran over to see the mule on

which he would ride. He seemed to forget his troubles, and didn't ask about his mother again. He seemed to know what had happened to his father without asking.

Al made a saddle out of a blanket, and "Uncle John" lifted Paul to the mule's back when the journey began again. When Paul laughed at the way the mule flicked its long ears, John felt that he was going to be all right. As the train moved on eastward, he and Paul grew to be close friends.

There was one more Indian attack, at Pawnee Rock, where the Arkansas River bends south and the trail leaves it. This time, the wagon train was not taken by surprise. No one was killed, and the attack did not last long. Ten days later, the train reached Independence, Missouri.

"What are you going to do with the boy?" the other trappers asked John, for the boy seemed to belong more to John than to any of the others.

"I have an aunt here in town. She is old and cannot care for him long, but she can keep him until I find another home for him," John said.

Bill went on to St. Louis, but John, Dick and Al stayed in Independence, planning to go west again. They planned to travel with the supply train which would be going west to Bent's Fort in about two months.

During the lazy days while they waited at Independence, John Smith spent many hours with Paul. One day he saw a pretty little black pony. He bought it for Paul, and fitted it with a saddle just the right size. He remembered a fine deerskin he had in his belongings, and took it to a shop where it was made into fringed leggings and a jacket for Paul. He found a white sombrero in another shop.

"He makes quite a picture," people said when they saw the boy dressed in his new clothes and riding his pony. "But Smith should take him to the orphans' home in St. Louis. An old trapper doesn't know how to take care of a little boy."

John knew that was what he should do. But he could not bring himself to do it. The day drew near when he and Al and Dick were to head west again. When they rode out of Independence, Paul rode his black pony beside John's big mule.

The Bent's Fort wagon train was a big one. There were seventy-five wagons, loaded with goods and groceries for the fort and for Santa Fe. Each wagon was pulled by a six-mule team and driven by teamsters who had covered the trail often. They saw Indians, but none chose to attack this big train. Little Paul and the three trappers had chosen a safe way to travel west.

It was near the end of September, and Bent's Fort was just ahead. The wagon train camped outside the fort just before suppertime that night.

"Come on, Paul," John said. "We're going to the fort to buy some milk for you."

Paul ran quickly to John and took his hand. The two went inside the fort and back to the big kitchens. There the women were busy tending the kettles of food cooking in the fireplaces. John was surprised to see that one of the cooks was a white woman, as he had seen only Indian women there before.

"Can we get some milk for the boy?" John called out. The white woman looked up. Instantly, she dropped her spoon and cried out, "Paul!"

"Mama!" cried Paul. "I knew I'd find you!"

John thought the woman would never stop hugging the boy.

"Well, I'll be danged," was all he could say.

When at last she remembered the man who had brought her boy to her, Paul's mother stood up and held out her hand to him. "I'll never be able to thank

you enough," she said, "no matter how long I live. I've prayed every day for this to happen! And Paul looks just wonderful. You must have taken good care of him."

She had to know all about what had happened that night after the Indian had carried her away. When she knew Paul's story, she told what had happened to her.

She had been taken to an Indian village. Carefully, she planned her escape. One night she had slipped away, riding a little iron-gray horse she had chosen ahead of time. She had to ride without a saddle, of course, but the pony carried her far from the village. She knew which way to go, for she had watched the direction of the sun on the way to the Indian village. She found the Santa Fe Trail and a wagon train going to Bent's Fort.

The men of Bent's Fort were full of good cheer that night, happy that Paul and his mother had come together again. They all gave money to help the two buy their way back east.

It was hard for John to say good-by to Paul on the day the boy and Mrs. Dale rode out of the fort. He had begun to think of Paul as his son. But he knew that a trapper's life was not the best thing for a small boy.

A trapper's life became too hard even for the men

who were used to it. Some of them took jobs as hunters for the outposts or for wagon trains or steamboats. Some were guides for travelers. A few became buffalo hunters. "Uncle John" Smith turned to catching wild horses and taming them to sell.

But the outposts were still needed. When New Mexico and all the southwest to the Pacific Ocean became part of the United States, travel and trade grew greater. Then gold was discovered in California and in other places in the west. Americans swarmed all over the Great Plains and the Rocky Mountains. The outposts had more business than ever.

The Indians saw the white men taking the land the government had said was theirs to keep. They became more and more angry and there were more raids on wagon trains. The United States government sent blue uniformed soldiers to the West to keep peace. The government built more forts for the soldiers, and bought many of the old trading posts.

The bugle call was heard all across the West. And all too often the call was "Boots and Saddles," calling the soldiers out to quiet an Indian war party. For fifteen or twenty years, the men of the cavalry manned the outposts, helping travelers go west in safety.

THE BOY WHO SAVED
FORT KEARNEY

By 1865, wagon train days were almost over. Old Jim Bridger found so few travelers coming his way after the War Between the States began that he gave up his outpost and joined the army as a scout. The Indian fighting was worse than ever, especially up in Wyoming, where Chief Red Cloud was trying to stop the white man from taking over his last good hunting grounds.

But the white man would not be stopped. Jim Bridger was asked to mark out a trail in Wyoming on which there would be a chain of forts, from Fort Laramie to the new gold fields at Virginia City, Montana. Fort Reno had been built and now the newest fort. Fort Phil Kearney on the Little Piney River was ready, too.

It was December 20, 1866. Each day, since early in July, a long train of wagons had left the new fort to go to a pine woods seven miles away. There the big crew of woodcutters cut the pine trees of which the fort had been built. On this December 20, the wagons were loaded with firewood. With the fort finished, only the winter's supply of firewood was still to be brought inside.

Young John Phillips pulled his mule team to a stop. The gates of Fort Phil Kearney were open, but John and the other woodcutters waited to let the patrol of soldiers ride into the fort.

Another mule team pulled up alongside John's. The driver pointed towards the end of the line of blue uniformed riders. "They had a bad day," he said. "Chief Red Cloud's boys are closing in on us."

John looked towards the end of the line of high stepping horses. A small group moved more slowly. One horse carried a man lying across the saddle. Two other soldiers were bent forward. John knew that some of the woodcutters had been fired upon that day, too.

"Colonel Carrington says no man should go out of sight of his patrol," John said. "It is a good thing the fort is finished. Jim Bridger said that war parties are gathering for miles around."

The last blue-uniformed man rode inside the fort.

"Gee-yup!" the drivers yelled, and the mules leaned into their harnesses to pull the heavily-loaded wagons inside the stockade.

Soon John had his team unhitched and was taking off the heavy harness. One of the young soldiers cared for his fine riding horse near by. As John started to work on his mules, he wished that for just one day he could care for one of those beautiful riding horses, as he had in the days when he carried the mail to Fort Laramie.

"How did it go today, Portugee?" the soldier asked.

"Portugee" was what most of the men called John. His family had come to America from Portugal and somehow had made their way to the wild west at the foot of the Rocky Mountains. They had built a trading post where the Powder River began, about where Fort Reno stood now. John had grown up in the shadow of the Big Horn Mountains, and he knew this part of the country almost as well as old Jim Bridger did.

John led his team to the water trough as he talked with the soldier. "The scouts saw a big war party, but only a few Indians came near us. They fired at some of the woodcutters, but no one was killed."

The soldier said, "Red Cloud is getting ready for something big. Each day we see signs of more Indians.

A small war party fired on us today and then rode off."

John thought of the soldier lying across the saddle. "Sometimes I wish I were in the army myself," he said. "I could do more than just cut wood."

The soldier gave his horse a last pat and turned to go. He said, "Don't do it Portugee. Your job as a woodcutter is almost finished. Get out while you can."

"I would be lost anywhere else," John said. He looked down at his dirty leather clothes and at his hands, hard from handling an ax and cracked from the cold of the December winds. He pushed back his long black hair and led his mules to their stall. It would be nice to wear a uniform, and have a pair of those big-cuffed leather gloves for his hands. But best of all, he would ride out each day on a beautiful horse.

The shadows of the Big Horn Mountains brought darkness to the fort early these December days. John lit a lantern and turned toward the bunkhouse. The woodcutters were getting into line with their tin plates and cups for the hot food the cook had ready.

December 21 began like any other day. Every woodcutter at the fort was ordered to go out, for this was to be the last day of getting firewood. A bigger guard than usual was sent with them, too.

Jim Bridger watched them go from the watchtower at the fort. He could see for miles. He saw the long line of wagons creep the seven miles to the Pinery. Just beyond the dark wooded slopes was Lodge Trail Ridge. The valley beyond the ridge was out of sight. Because Colonel Carrington, commander of Fort Phil Kearney, knew that the war parties were all around, he had ordered a guard to be kept on a rise called Pilot Hill, too. If Indian trouble came, the message would come to the fort by signal flags. If the signaler rode his horse in a circle as he waved the flags, it would mean "Many Indians are attacking the wood train!"

About noon the signal came.

"Lt. Col. Fetterman, ready your detail!" ordered Col. Carrington.

Lt. Col. Fetterman had been in the West for only a short time. He had often been heard to say, "If I had eighty men, I could wipe out Red Cloud's war party!" Old Jim Bridger shook his head when he heard this.

"These young fellers don't know anything about Indian fighting!" he said, and Col. Carrington knew Jim was right.

The breath of the waiting cavalrymen and their

horses rose like a steamy cloud. The frozen ground rang with the pawing of the horses. Colonel Carrington realized, as he checked the detail of men, that he had given Lt. Col. Fetterman exactly eighty men.

"Your duty is to support the wood-train guard," he told the young officer. "No soldier is to cross Lodge Trail Ridge. That is an order."

Lt. Col. Fetterman saluted and rode away with his eighty men. In the watch tower, Jim Bridger saw them ride towards the Pinery. After a while, from far off, came the sound of firing. Col. Carrington watched with Jim.

"I can't see Fetterman's detail at all," he said.

Jim shook his head. "Last I saw, they were heading for Lodge Trail Ridge, Colonel. That feller over on Pilot Hill is signaling his head off, sir."

The colonel quickly left the tower. A few minutes later, almost every soldier in the fort was riding off toward Lodge Trail Ridge. From the top, they looked down at the plain on the other side. Lt. Col. Fetterman had ridden his men over the ridge and into a trap in the valley below. There were a thousand warriors, and no sign of a living blue uniformed cavalryman.

That night, the temperature dropped fast. "A blizzard is coming, mark my words," Jim Bridger said.

The chill in the air was matched by the chill in the hearts of the people of Fort Kearney. Colonel Carrington was sure that Red Cloud would strike at the fort, knowing there were eighty less men to hold it.

"All women and children are to stay inside the powder house," he ordered. It was the strongest building in the fort.

Woodcutter John Phillips, with some of the other men, worked at spiking heavy beams into place to make the walls stronger. Some of his anger went into each blow with the heavy hammer. He heard a baby crying inside the powder house, and thought of the baby's father—the young soldier who had talked with him the night before. He had been one of those who followed Lt. Col. Fetterman over Lodge Trail Ridge.

A bugle call brought all the men together in the open square in the center of the fort. Woodcutters and soldiers listened as Col. Carrington talked of the danger all of them faced. The biting cold wind thinned his voice, and John moved in closer to hear, blinking his eyes against the first snowflakes the wind carried.

"Our only hope is to get men from Fort Laramie,"

the colonel said. "But it is more than two hundred miles southwest of here, a long and dangerous ride through rough country patrolled by Red Cloud's men. Someone must go. It is our hope, our only hope, of saving the women and children in that room."

All eyes turned toward the powder house. Many of the soldiers had loved ones in there whom they did not want to leave to face Indian attack without them.

The colonel spoke again. "Someone must go," he said.

John put down the heavy hammer he still held. "I'll go, Colonel Carrington," he said. "Give me a good horse to ride, and I'll go."

The colonel faced the dark-eyed young man. "Portugee, you are not in the army. I cannot order you to make this ride. You know you may never return from it."

"You can spare me better than a soldier. And I've ridden this trail before, when I carried the mail." John said.

The colonel held out his hand. "You will be doing the greatest thing a man was ever called on to do. Now come with me and we'll get a message ready."

It was about midnight when John left the fort.

He was dressed in the warmest clothes which could be found. He had buffalo boots on his feet, a heavy buffalo coat, and a fur cap pulled well over his ears. Even so, he could feel the bite of the twenty-five-degrees-below-zero air.

In his saddlebags he had a few biscuits for himself and some feed for the horse he was to ride, the colonel's own fine riding horse. Each man's hopes went with him as he rode out the gate, but few believed he had a chance to make the long ride.

The few flakes of snow had become the blizzard Jim Bridger had promised. Already the snow was drifting against the stockade walls as John started out. He rode on, guiding the horse more from memory of the trail than from sight. But with the gray light of morning he left the trail to find shelter for himself and the horse. He would have to hide until dark, for Red Cloud's men would be sure to see a lone rider against the snow.

He did not dare build a fire. He pulled evergreen boughs about himself and the horse, and huddled all day against a rocky cliff. When, at last, he tried to get on the horse again, he was so stiff he could hardly make it.

The blizzard had not yet ended. The horse had to pick its way through four foot drifts. At other times, the trail was an open, icy path, swept clean by the bitter cold winds.

That night, soldiers lying in their bunks at Fort Reno heard the guard call the hour of midnight. Before sleep had carried them away again, they came wide awake at the sound of a call at the gate.

"Message from Colonel Carrington!" they heard, and then the heavy gates creaked. Those who looked out their doors saw a creature that looked like a snowman slide stiffly from a heaving horse. The "snowman" went into the commanding officer's quarters.

In a few minutes, word spread through Fort Reno of what had happened at Fort Phil Kearney to the north. The commander ordered a fresh horse saddled for John, again the best horse the post had. The messenger refused to stay in the fort the rest of the night, but was back in the saddle as soon as the horse was ready.

By the third night, John was so cold that he could hardly move the reins to guide the horse around the deepest drifts. But he knew that Horseshoe Station was only a few miles ahead.

The colonel had told him, "The telegraph wires have reached Horseshoe Station, and they connect with Fort Laramie. The telegraph operator will send the message on, and you will not need to go any farther."

The horse was very tired. John thought the animal was going to stop altogether as they reached the edge of the open prairie in which Horseshoe Station stood. He could not blame the animal for wanting to turn its back to the wind and find shelter.

"Come on, boy," he urged. "Only a little farther and then both of us can rest."

Just then, he heard a war cry. It came from the top of the ridge behind him. John dug his booted heels into the horse's sides, and the animal put all its strength into the last run across the open stretch in which the station stood. John thought he heard hoof-beats behind him, but as he pulled to a stop at the station there was no sign of anyone following him.

"They know I'm armed," the surprised telegraph operator told him. "Besides, Indians don't like to fight at night or in the cold. Get your horse into the stall and come on in."

One minute later, the operator was clicking out the call to Fort Laramie. He waited then for some sign that the message was getting through. None came.

"Rest awhile, fellow," he said to John. "I don't know whether the wires have come down in the storm, or if the Fort Laramie operator is asleep." He went on tapping his call and then waiting for an answer.

John was pulling on his fur gloves. "Do you have a spare horse?" he asked.

The telegraph operator looked up. "You aren't going out there again, are you? Rest your horse and yourself. I have no horse to let you take. The only one out there is lame."

But John was already on his way out. There were forty miles still to go. He could make ten more miles before daylight.

He spent Christmas Eve day huddled in the cold again. That night, just before midnight, he saw ahead the dark shadows of the great walls of Fort Laramie. The old fur-trading post had been rebuilt as an adobe fort since the government had bought it. It was the largest military post in all that part of the West.

John's horse seemed to sense that inside those high white walls was journey's end. He broke into a gallop, and the sound of his hoofbeats on the windswept frozen ground brought out a guard.

"Who goes there?" called the guard.

"Message from Colonel Carrington," John's stiff lips could hardly shape the words, but the surprised guard let horse and rider in and hurried to open the inner gate, too.

A soldier took his horse's bridle and John slid from the animal's back. He half walked, half fell toward the building to which the guard led him. Lights shone from its windows. Even through his covering of fur and ice, John could hear sounds of music and laughter.

"The Christmas Eve party," the soldier explained. Then he opened the door to the clubhouse.

The sounds died. The dancing people turned to stare at the strange figure in the doorway. It was as if a ghostly Jack Frost had come to the party.

The commanding officer hurried toward the stranger. John pulled off a glove and reached inside his coat for Colonel Carrington's message. As he pulled it out, he fell forward.

The women of Fort Laramie took care of "Portugee" John in the days that followed. As soon as he knew what was going on around him, they told him of the soldiers who had set out for Fort Phil Kearney on Christmas Day. But when John asked about the horse which had carried him all the way from Fort Reno, the news was not good. Fort Laramie had been a true "journey's end" for the fine animal. It, too, had fallen to the ground, but the soldiers had not been able to save its life.

Then, at last, the word John waited for came over the repaired telegraph wires. The blizzard which had made John's journey so hard had been a blessing in disguise, for it had held off the attack on Fort Phil Kearney until help came.

To the people of the northern fort, "Portugee" John was no longer just a woodcutter. He was a hero.

WILD BILL HICKOK, ARMY SCOUT

The days of the old mountain men were ending. The new army scouts were the men who had worked for the freight and passenger wagon companies in their days of learning about the West. That was how Wild Bill Hickok, one of the last of the scouts, got his chance to go west.

Wild Bill wasn't "Wild Bill" when he left his home town in Illinois to go west. He was James Butler Hickok. He came to be called *Wild Bill* years later.

Bill went to work for one of the stagecoach companies in 1858, when he was twenty-one years old. It was the same company which had hired little eleven-year-old Billy Cody the year before. Billy Cody, who would someday be famous as *Buffalo Bill,* thought big Bill Hickok was the dashing kind of stage driver he'd like to be himself. The two became friends, and their paths crossed many times in later years.

Bill Hickok had his hero, too. He had read all the stories he could find about Kit Carson. When the stage company sent him out to Santa Fe, Bill Hickok saw his hero in one of the inns. He pulled together all his courage and walked over to Kit.

"Colonel Carson," he said, "I've read a lot about you, and I'd sure like to shake your hand. My name's Hickok—I drive the stage."

Kit Carson, who was a rancher in those days, stood up. Bill Hickok was surprised to see how small his hero was. He, himself, was over six feet tall with broad shoulders. Kit was neither tall nor broad of shoulder. But the young stage driver admired him all the more for the things he had done.

Kit held out his leathery hand. He liked the looks of this young fellow.

"Sit down," he said, and a friendship began. Before Bill had left Santa Fe again, Kit had taken him all around town. Bill could hardly believe his good luck.

It may have been some of Kit's courage that passed to Bill Hickok and saved his life a short time later. His stage company owned wagons which carried goods all over the west. In 1860, Bill was made wagonmaster of a freight wagon train which traveled the mountain road between Santa Fe and the area where Bent's Fort had stood until the day it was blown up in 1852. To get there, the wagons had to go through the Raton Pass, which Kit Carson had traveled many and many a time.

There was one especially bad part of the trail through the pass. The wagons had to go one at a time and very slowly. Bill's job was to see that all the wagons got through safely, so he rode up and down the length of the wagon train and helped one wagon at a time get through the bad place.

On that day in 1860, he guided one wagon through the pass and turned to go back to meet the next one. He was on a lonely stretch where the trail passed through a pine woods when he saw a big mother grizzly bear come onto the trail just ahead of him. She was going to make sure that her two cubs, hidden in the pines, were kept safe.

"Whoa, there!" Bill cried as his horse reared. But the horse was too frightened to quiet down. She threw Bill from the saddle and ran back down the trail.

Bill was shaken by his fall, but there was no time to lie there with the bear charging toward him. He got to his feet as quickly as he could. His rifle was in the holster on his saddle, but he had a revolver and a knife with him. He pulled the revolver out and fired at the oncoming bear.

His shot rang out. Bill was sure he hit the bear, but she just shook her head and kept coming. He fired again, and then a third time. She kept coming.

As she rose to her hind legs to attack him, Bill emptied his revolver into the great bear. She snarled horribly and those terrible jaws were so close that he could feel the bear's breath.

The beast reached for Bill with spread claws. Bill felt his arm being ripped as he pulled his knife from his belt. He must get it into her before she could squeeze him to death. He struggled and pushed as he tried to turn the blade toward her chest. As she pulled him close, the knife point touched and went into the bear. Man and beast fell to the ground together.

The last thing Bill heard was the bear's bellow as they fell. When the next wagon came up, the driver found Bill and pulled him from under the bear.

It was months before Bill was well enough to work again, but slowly he grew strong again.

When the War Between the States began, Bill left

the wagon company to join the fighting. He was a scout and a spy for the Union Army, taking part in the fighting in southwestern Missouri and north-western Arkansas. By the time the war was over, he had won his name of *Wild Bill*.

He had also won a beautiful horse as a prize of war. He named her *Black Nell,* and she obeyed his every command perfectly. He took to wearing fine clothes about that time, and let his hair fall in long waves to his shoulders. He was quite a handsome figure riding about on beautiful Black Nell. He rode her west in 1868 to take a job as an army scout at the new outposts in western Kansas and Colorado. Buffalo Bill was a scout in the same command.

One Sunday afternoon in September, 1868, Bill was on his way back to his headquarters at Fort Lyon in Colorado. He had been sent to Fort Hays in Kansas with messages. He was in no special hurry as he rode along on Black Nell on the return trip, and when he saw an overturned covered wagon he got off his horse to look it over.

As he drew near, he saw that the wagon was partly burned. Then he saw several dead bodies.

"Another Indian attack on a wagon train," he thought.

Bill made sure that there was no living person near. Then he rode on. He reached a little town about an hour later. One of the men there hailed him.

"Did you see any signs of Indians?"

Wild Bill said, "I saw where they had been." He told the man about the wagon.

"We're getting a party ready to ride out to try to find the Indians that attacked the train," the man said. "Can you join us?"

Wild Bill decided he could, and when thirty-four men had gathered to ride against the Indians, Bill rode with them. They asked him to be their leader. None of them were trained soldiers, and they brought whatever guns they had. Some of them were the kind the mountain men had brought with them. A few had the new rifles which could be reloaded quickly.

For eight days, the men searched the countryside for the band of Cheyennes who, they were sure, had attacked the wagon train. They were heading back to the settlement, ready to give up the chase because they were low on food and ammunition when they sighted the Indians.

Wild Bill and a few others had climbed to the top of a table-shaped rise of land called a mesa, to look over the countryside. Ahead of them and below was a broad plain.

"There they are!" cried Bill. On the plain were camped several hundred Indians.

"They've spotted us, too!" cried one of the men. "They're pointing this way!"

Wild Bill knew they were in trouble. He gave orders quickly. "Everybody get up here on the mesa, and bring your horses. Start digging trenches so that we are walled in. We'll have a fight on our hands soon."

While a few stood guard, the rest started digging in the sandy soil. They had no shovels and had to use spurs, tin cups, plates or spoons. It was slow work, but they dug out about a dozen holes and piled the dirt between them and the mesa's edge. The holes were large enough to hide the men and those horses that were not hit by the first shots when the attack began, for the Cheyennes sent their first round of shots before the holes were finished.

Wild Bill had a gun loaded with buckshot. He and the other frontiersmen were all "crack shots." Each time the Cheyennes made a dash around the mesa, one or more fell to the ground. The firing went on all afternoon.

When darkness came, Bill called a council.

"We're in real trouble, men. Someone may be able to slip down to the creek during the night to get water, but our food is almost gone. Worse, our ammunition won't last another hour of fighting."

The men were silent. In a moment Bill went on. "Black Nell and I are going to leave here in a few minutes. If we make it through the Indian lines, we'll ride for help. I think we're near enough to the village for me to make it there and back here before daylight. Wish us luck!"

Bill loaded his revolvers and tucked them into his belt. He jumped onto Black Nell, and a moment later the men heard the sound of falling bits of stone as the horse dashed down the slope. Then there were shots.

"Did they get him?" one of the men breathed. But a moment later they heard the cracking of Bill's revolver, and the pounding of Black Nell's hoofs went on until the sound was lost in the distance.

It was forty-five miles to the little settlement where the thirty-four waiting men on the mesa lived. Bill, letting Black Nell run at her own pace, could only hope that she would not step into a gopher hole or stumble on a rock. Luck was with man and horse, and they thundered into the village.

Bill yelled, "Hey, ther-rr-re! Wake up!" and heads popped out of windows and answered in the darkness.

"We need every man we can get to ride to save your men!" Bill called. Each of the six men, who hurried into his clothes and came out to the street with his horse, rode farther out to get another. Most of the men of the village were in the little band of thirty-four out on the mesa.

In an hour, a dozen men were ready to follow Bill. While they gathered, Bill had been let into the store by the storekeeper. He had a big sack of food and ammunition tied behind his saddle.

"Follow me, boys!" he cried. "This is a ride for life!"

Thirteen horses pounded over the trail back to the mesa.

There was no time to spare, for the Indians must

not see how very small was the band of rescuers. To get to the mesa while darkness lasted was their only hope.

When they were almost there, Bill called a halt.

"When we reach the plain, I'll yell," he said. "All of you scream and yell as if you were a hundred men instead of a dozen. We'll charge across the plain, yelling, and ride onto the mesa without stopping."

"Unless we are stopped," one of the men said softly. But he and all the others urged their horses forward as Black Nell moved silently on. They would be as quiet as possible until they were right upon the plain.

"Yee-ow!" yelled Bill, suddenly, and Black Nell galloped as fast as she could go.

"Yee-OW, YEE-OW!" yelled all the others. The men on the mesa wondered how Bill had found a hundred men in their little settlement.

The Indians, awakened from their sleep by the sound of such fierce yells and pounding hoofs, thought the whole United States Army was riding in upon them. They did the first thing they thought of. They ran, under cover of the little darkness that was left.

Dawn came. The forty-seven men on the mesa

lay ready to fire at the first charge. As daylight came over the plain, they saw that the Indian camp was gone.

Forty-six men of that tiny Colorado village never forgot their dangerous adventure with bold, dashing Wild Bill Hickok. As for Bill himself, he went on to Fort Lyon, soon to be the hero of another adventure and another and another, for that was his way of life.

But even as Wild Bill rode around the plains on Black Nell, the Indians began to face the fact that they must share their west with the white man. The puffing Iron Horse was moving mile by mile across the plains and over the mountains. Villages, like the one in Colorado, and then cities took the place of lonely outposts.

But here and there a rotted log or a crumbling adobe wall told of the days when the West was wild and lonely, and a man had to be a hero to stay alive.